Benjamin Peirce, Henry Mitchell

The Harbor of New York

It's Condition, May 1873

Benjamin Peirce, Henry Mitchell

The Harbor of New York
It's Condition, May 1873

ISBN/EAN: 9783744734295

Printed in Europe, USA, Canada, Australia, Japan

Cover: Foto ©ninafisch / pixelio.de

More available books at **www.hansebooks.com**

THE HARBOR OF NEW-YORK:

ITS CONDITION, MAY, 1873.

LETTER OF PROF. BENJAMIN PEIRCE,

Superintendent of the United States Coast Survey,

TO THE

Chamber of Commerce of New-York,

WITH THE

REPORT OF PROF. HENRY MITCHELL,

ON THE

PHYSICAL SURVEY OF THE HARBOR.

PRINTED BY ORDER OF THE CHAMBER OF COMMERCE.

New-York:
PRESS OF THE CHAMBER OF COMMERCE.
1873.

JOHN W. AMERMAN, PRINTER,
No. 47 Cedar Street, N. Y.

THE HARBOR OF NEW-YORK.

At the meeting of the Chamber of Commerce, held on the 5th of June, 1873, the following letter from Professor BENJAMIN PEIRCE, Superintendent of the United States Coast Survey, with the accompanying report on the Physical Survey of the Harbor of New-York, by Prof. HENRY MITCHELL, were submitted by Mr. GEORGE W. Dow, Chairman of the Special Committee appointed by the Chamber to confer with the Superintendent on this subject. The letter and report were ordered to be printed for distribution:

CAMBRIDGE, MASS., May 30th, 1873.

Dear Sir:

The resolution passed in the Chamber of Commerce March 4, 1869, has been under careful consideration during the interval which has elapsed, and a continuous investigation of all the phenomena of New-York Harbor has been conducted under the direction of Professor HENRY MITCHELL, to whom the physical hydrography of the survey has been especially entrusted.

The enclosed report from Professor MITCHELL illustrates the character and progress of the survey up to the present time. In it important numerical data are skillfully arranged, and in many cases exhibited in the forms of diagrams. All these data may be regarded as final, as far as they go, and it should be especially considered that nothing in the report is speculative, or merely theoretical. The paper is an embodiment of facts and observation. It is systematic experience, which is the most valuable as it is the most fruitful experience. The deductions are not from prejudice or unfounded fancy; they result from careful study and inquiry by men who are familiar with New-York Harbor and with the general laws of the dynamic action of waves, tides and currents. The observers have sought the opinions of pilots, ship captains and engineers, and have neglected nothing which could conduce to a judicious conclusion. Wherever, therefore, injury to the harbor is specified, there can be no doubt that the proper remedy should be applied without unnecessary delay, and no undertaking can wisely be pressed in reference to the harbor that is manifestly opposite to the teachings of observation developed in this report of Professor MITCHELL.

It will be observed that the Jersey Flats no longer receive the deposits formerly carried by currents upon its interior space. The extensions of wharves, etc., at Jersey City have placed the flats under the lee, and the deposits now accumulate on the fore slope of the bank, so that the flats are rapidly growing out into the main channel. In large measure these deposits are dredgings brought down from the city docks and elsewhere, but some of the material found on them is still to be accounted for. Any scheme of occupation for these flats should provide specially for keeping the frontage bold, and the harbor line should not lie far back from the present front of the flats.

In the vicinity of Middle Ground Shoal, and of Gowanus, a similar movement outward seems to have resulted from the artificial encroachments at Red Hook, but there the accumulation from foreign sources is small, and the changes observed have not been permanent.

There is no indication that the bar channels have declined in any way. These will be reached by the survey last of all, unless something should appear to attract attention to them in advance.

The Lower Bay anchorage has changed, and this has been examined, but a further extension of work and close soundings are desirable there before results can be declared.

Mr. MITCHELL's observations relative to the sub-current up the Hudson River develope the interesting fact that the flood predominates below six fathoms.

The depth on the bar is about equal to the seaward scour through the harbor, namely, 22 feet at low water; but this does not depend upon density, nor has it directly to do with dead angle.

Professor MITCHELL gives good reasons for preferring *middle time* in the East River to the time of high or low water as that to be given to navigators; first, because it is less liable to fluctuation from accidental causes, and then it is nearer the time of most rapid velocity, which is especially of importance to the sailor.

The whole amount of water which flows into New-York Harbor in the course of each tide through the East River is sufficient of itself to raise the water of the harbor by one foot and one-tenth. If this flow from the East River into the harbor occupied the whole of ebb time, it would increase by just this amount the outer flow through the Narrows and over the bar, and the ratio which this water bears to the whole outer flow would exactly represent the benefit of the East River in preserving the depth of water over the bar of the harbor. But this coincidence does not exactly occur. The ebb commences two hours before the turn of the tide in the East River, and during these two hours the flow is towards the East River instead of from it. Hence the amount of flow into the harbor must be proportionally diminished and reduced to nine-tenths (.9) of a foot. Now the harbor at high tide has four and two-tenths (4.2) feet more of water in it than at low tide, which runs out during the ebb, together with the flow from the Hudson, which is about the same as that of East River. The whole of the flow, then, through the Narrows, which is independent of East River, corresponds to five and three-tenths (5.3) feet in elevation of the surface of the harbor, and this is the amount which would run if East River were to be cut off. The additional nine-tenths (.9) of a foot which arises from East River, gives a total of six and two-tenths (6.2) feet as representing the flow through the Narrows and over the bar. If the East River were cut off, the corresponding decrease in the flow of water would involve a proportionate decrease in the water space over the bar, or a reduction of the depth of water upon the bar of about three feet and a half.* Such is the measure of the importance of East River to the preservation of the entrance to New-York Harbor. The loss of this river would involve a fatal injury to the harbor, and any obstruction to its flow or reduction of its capacity must be proportionally injurious.

Believing that the accompanying report embraces the principal points which deserve immediate attention, it is respectfully presented for the consideration of the Chamber of Commerce, and I hope that it will be considered to deserve immediate publication.

Yours respectfully,

BENJAMIN PEIRCE,
Superintendent U. S. Coast Survey.

GEO. W. DOW, Esq.,
Chairman.

---

* This is a result of a simple application of the rule of three. The reduction of the depth upon the bar must bear the same proportion to the mean depth of 24.2 feet, which the diminution of the flow of water represented by .9 bears to the whole flow represented by 6.2, *i. e.*, the reduction must be a little more than one-seventh part, or more exactly 3½ feet—for the water-way must evidently correspond in magnitude to the amount of water which flows through it.—B. P.

REPORT BY PROF. HENRY MITCHELL

TO THE

SUPERINTENDENT OF THE U. S. COAST SURVEY.

May 6th, 1873.

DEAR SIR :

The Physical Survey of New-York Harbor and its approaches was resumed in 1871, and has made, during the past two years, considerable progress, so that some results can be stated quite safely. The immediate occasion of the resumption of these inquiries was a resolution of the New-York Chamber of Commerce, dated March 4th, 1869, calling upon you to consider " an apparent change going " on in the formation of the harbor of New-York and its entrance, " which, if not soon attended to and corrected, threatens to be pro- " ductive of very great injury."

You, in reply, named Capt. C. P. PATTERSON and myself as your associates in the study suggested, and asked for a committee of conference, which was at once appointed by the Chamber, and has been retained up to this time. This arrangement has been a great advantage to me, since it has given me, in field operations, a claim upon your special interest, and the co-operation of Capt. PATTERSON. I have also felt free to consult Mr. DOW and Mr. BLUNT, (of the Committee,) from time to time, and thus the work has been more closely confined to practical objects and wants than it was in our first attempt 15 years ago.

You will not, of course, expect, in this progress report, any general discussion. I am, in fact, not prepared for this, but I shall take up certain shoals and channels, and state facts regarding their changes and conditions of existence as far as we have learned them.

Changes for the worse being the most important, I shall commence with them; but, in order that our facts may not produce an exaggerated impression, I feel that it is necessary to say, beforehand, that no evidence of a *general deterioration of the port* has yet appeared, and that we see no reason to apprehend any further decline of commercial facilities if wise counsels prevail in future.

INCREASE OF JERSEY FLATS.

In the autumn of 1872 the survey of Jersey Flats was completed by Mr. MARINDIN and his party, and the figures given in the appended tables are those resulting from a comparison of the recent survey with that of 1855, which has been replotted at Washington under the special care of Capt. PATTERSON, who has advised with us in these surveys from the first.

The plan of comparison we have pursued has been as follows :— A line has been drawn upon our field sheet from Robbins' Reef Light-House to Bedloe's Island flagstaff, thence slightly deflecting through Ellis' Island flagstaff to the New-Jersey Central R. R. wharf. This datum line lies above all marked changes, and is so placed as to fall nearly parallel to the border of the flats, so that ordinates from it are essentially normals to the characteristic contours upon the bank of the main channel. (See Diagram A.) We have drawn 38 of these normals between Robbins' Reef Light and the Central R. R., at distances of 500 feet ; and at the turn into the channel leading to the Kills, we have constructed radii from the Light-House as a centre. Upon these normals we have measured the changes in the positions of the 6, 12, 18, 24 and 30 feet curves since 1855, and stated our results numerically upon Table I. This first table shows the advance or retreat of the contours at the points where they are intersected by the normals. You will observe that all the curves have been pushed outwards since 1855, but most conspicuously the 24 feet curve, which, in the average, has moved out 303 feet, and, at the maximum, 825 feet. By just so much the main channel of the harbor, for heavy ships, has been reduced in width. The extreme reduction stated, however, equals only one-sixth part of the former width of the channel.

In this neighborhood deposits of material dredged from the city docks and elsewhere had been made for many years previous to 1871, when, at our suggestion, the Pilot Commission declined to grant the privilege of further deposits. As I understand the matter, this Commission had designated as a site for deposit the deep waters of the main channel off Oyster Island, where our printed map showed depths of over 10 fathoms. Whether or not the parties who dumped the material were careless of their whereabouts, and found it more convenient to drop their loads on the border of the flats, we are not advised; but we feel pretty sure, from the aspect of the case, that the great shoaling in this place is artificial.

The greatest elevation of deposit since our survey of 1855 is 31½ feet, reducing to 4 feet depth a portion of the main Ship Channel, where some 17 years ago the Great Eastern could have passed with 250 feet between her and the 30 feet curve. The foregoing is an extreme case, of course; but we are able to state that the flats, throughout the entire distance from Robbins' Reef to normal XXXIII., a distance of over three statute miles, have grown out into the Main Channel to the injury of navigation. Some excavations— and deposits incidental to these excavations—seem to have disturbed the order of things between Ellis' Island and the Central Rail-Road Wharf, so that no general statement can be safely made concerning the change in the area of the flats in this particular neighborhood.

If we regard the 24 feet contour as being the true border of the flats on the side towards the Main Channel, we may state the increase of the shoal ground to be 129 acres. Next in magnitude of change, and most important from a commercial point of view, is the outward movement of the 18 feet curve, which amounts in the average to 211 feet, and represents over 92 acres.

Upon normal XVII., (the dumping ground above referred to,) the maximum movement outwards is 930 feet, and upon adjacent normals, on either hand, 710 feet. The 12 feet curve has advanced to a still greater extent on normal XVII., where it is found to be over a thousand feet further out than in 1855!

The 6 feet curve is so near the general plane of the surface of the flats that its movements are on the whole uncertain and insignificant. All the movements stated above are those which have taken place outside (seaward) of the axial line from which our normals are drawn. Within this line the nearly horizontal surface of the flats has remained essentially the same where unoccupied.

At the point of the flats near Robbins' Reef the border of the shoal ground has retreated over a hundred feet, except along the 12 feet curve, where little change has occurred. (See Table No. 2.)

In Table No. 3 I have furnished in detail the areas of change upon planes of 6, 12, 18, 24 and 30 feet depths at low water.

Finally, in Table No. 4, I furnish the volumes which have been added since 1855.

You will observe that nowhere along the front of the flats has there been any *loss*, but in every reach of a thousand feet a considerable *gain*—not less than 1,540,000 cubic feet in any case. The total deposit upon the border of the main channel since 1855 is 76,859,250 cubic feet, or 2,846,640 cubic yards. To dig out this mud again, and carry it where it could be of no possible harm, would cost nearly a million of dollars. This is rather a startling disclosure, when you consider the narrow belt that our figures cover. It is, however, less alarming than the result of the previous comparison made by the Advisory Council to the New-York Commissioners on Harbor Encroachments, in 1855–'57, but it is *more certain*, because we have the survey of that Council for our basis, and have proceeded as carefully ourselves in repeating the survey.

That Council pointed out as a cause of deposits the unwise extension of piers at Jersey City, but their warning voices were unheard or unheeded. As I have stated, much of the recent deposit appears to have been artificial, but there is enough unaccounted for to warrant an appeal to the State of New-Jersey to adopt measures for preventing unwise encroachments hereafter.

Changes in Buttermilk Channel.

In my report of last year, printed by the Pilot Commissioners as an Appendix to your letter to the President of the Board, bearing date of February 16, 1872, I described the results from a comparison of surveys made in Buttermilk Channel and over the shallow ground southward of Governor's Island. The only striking point stated was the diminution of depth on the summit of the shoal at the eastern entrance of this channel. Capt. Patterson has discovered in overhauling the records that a sounding of 9½ feet was made on this very spot in 1855, and omitted from the plotting— perhaps intentionally, after diligent search for the place had failed to repeat the observation. It is a very small knoll, and therefore difficult to find.

Changes in the vicinity of Middle Ground Shoal and Gowanus Bay.

The eastern side of the harbor, below the Atlantic Docks, was re-surveyed during the past season by Mr. F. F. Nes and his party, of the steamer Arago. The funds for this work were mostly supplied by the Commissioners on the Pier Lines of Brooklyn, for whose use our chart was made; but we have instituted a close comparison between this survey and the one of 1855. The method of comparison which I have adopted in this case, and shall describe below, differs from that employed for Jersey Flats, you will perceive, and you will easily see that in each case it is intended to make prominent the character of the change. In one instance, a flat is growing out into a deep channel, in the other the bottom is shifting; in the former the horizontal area and the volume are most important, in the latter the vertical changes of depth attract our attention.

Upon our field sheet we have drawn a straight line from the New-York City Hall, tangent to Red Hook, which terminates at Bay Ridge flag-staff. This line, which we may consider the outer chord of Gowanus Bay, we have made our axis of ordinates, and drawn these ordinates at intervals of 500 feet. We have also drawn parallels to our chord at distances of 250 feet, and at the points where these cross the ordinates we have determined the changes of depth, and stated the same in Table No. 7 and Diagram B. It was only by thus cutting up the ground into equal spaces that we could ascertain with any certainty the total deposit from foreign sources, and distinguish between *accumulation* and *shifting*. The general result is a shoaling, which on the harbor side of our chord is in the average only a quarter of a foot, and in Gowanus Bay, exclusive of the Erie Basin, less than a half foot. The Erie Basin itself, notwithstanding considerable dredging, is in the average 0.01 feet shoaler now than in 1855.

Referring to this diagram, you will discover that there has been a deepening off Red Hook, which we follow along the chord of the bay, and down two parallels on either side of this chord, *as if a stream had swept around Red Hook and across the opening of the bay, washing away the bottom irregularly.* It may be that the completion of wharves, extending from Red Hook, has quickened the stream from above a little and changed somewhat its direction. You will remember that I reported to you, (as member of the Commission on Pier Lines,) some time since, the causes of the Middle Ground as observed, and predicted that if Red Hook were extended this shoal would move out. I had not then made the comparison, and was not aware that any movement of importance had already taken place. You may trace in the groups of figures outside of the shoal upon our diagram a decided movement towards the Main Channel, and at the foot of the shoal the growth to the south-westward is striking.

The lower mouth of the Middle Ground Channel *(off Bay Ridge) seems to have had a shifting bottom, but no harmful change has

---

* Sometimes called the Owl's Head Channel.

taken place in this neighborhood. The bar of this channel, which lies between normals XVII. and XXII., and between parallels 500 and 2,000, (see Diagram B.,) has shoaled *nearly a foot in the average*, and there are places upon it which have *three and four feet less water* than formerly.

CHANGES AT AND NEAR THE SANDY HOOK ENTRANCE.

Our re-surveys have been confined, thus far, to localities where changes are reported or suspected, and the Sandy Hook Basin has been under examination with some interesting results; but until we can so extend the work as to comprise a wider range than that covered by the hydrography of Mr. NES, last autumn, I do not feel ready to discuss this part of my subject. I presume Mr. NES will join me again the coming season and complete this work. The west side of the Lower Bay, as far as examined in our surveys for the Department of Docks, had undergone no change worth mentioning.

TIDES AND CURRENTS.

Although I have not yet made all the observations requisite for a complete view of the tidal phenomena in the harbor and approaches of New-York, I have reached that point where I can exhibit my results in tables, complete as far as they go, and therefore I have thought best to ask you to accept these data, and have them printed, that they may be accessible to those persons whose public or private interests lead them to follow us in these inquiries. I have very great confidence in the accuracy of our observations. Messrs. H. L. MARINDIN and J. W. WEIR, of the Coast Survey, who practically led the observers, are known to you as careful officers, and they had for assistantss elected students from the Massachusetts Institute of Technology and the Troy Scientific School. I regret very much that the observations made by Mr. STRIEDINGER for Major-General NEWTON, could not be incorporated with our own in this report. They were kindly tendered by the General, but did not come to hand in season.

I shall commence by introducing tables showing at what interval after the transit of the moon the strength of the current occurs. I call this the *lunar-tidal interval of Middle Time*, because I do not use the time of the highest velocity recorded, but the middle of the curve, (for flood or for ebb,) given by all the velocities carefully plotted. This plan suggested itself to me when working on the currents of San Francisco, where the *diurnal inequalities** are very large, and the effects of freshets and prevailing winds very considerable. I concluded, that because the diurnal inequalities in the intervals of high and low water have different signs, the time of any intermediate phenomenon (like maximum velocity) must be more or less free of this inequality. Moreover, I concluded that the maximum velocity would occur at the same time, whatever constants might enter, so that, in great measure, this time would be unaffected by regular winds or continued river floods. In the case of San Francisco, my computations came out indifferently; but in treating New-York, the advantage of using *middle time* instead of slack water, is very decided. My method is illustrated in Fig. 1 of Diagram C., in which the observed curve is plotted in full line, while the chords and the axis are given in dotted lines. The mean time of the axis (which is a line drawn downwards, so as to bisect all the chords) is what we call the "*middle time*." You will observe, that this element is dependent upon all the observations, and not upon one or two, which might be the very ones affected by irregular causes. Table No. 8 contains the numerical dated from which the first figure upon our sketch is plotted; and Tables Nos. 9, 10 and 11 furnish all the principal elements of the tides and tidal currents. Tables 9 and 11 furnish the results from actual observations, while Table No. 10 is a recapitulation of Table No. 9, *adjusted* and extended. This adjustment is effected by plotting the observed results, and drawing through the figures smooth curves, which are supposed to strike out only those irregularities which have been due to strictly local peculiarities and errors of observation. The vertical tides, *i. e.*, the *rise and fall*, have required very little adjustment, because, being observed for long series, they give, from averages, a smooth curve. Our manner of observing the vertical tide, by recording the times of high and low water, and referring these to the moon's transit, is far less certain of giving the truth from short series of observations, than our method of using *middle time*, in the case of currents, or even the use of slackwater intervals; but the convenience with which the rise and fall of the tide can be observed, enables us to repeat observations till the mean results come very near to the truth.

To the adjusted table (10) we have added columns of deflections,

---

* Difference between morning and evening tides.

depths, sections, perimeters, mean radius, &c. ; all the elements which might be expected to vary the tidal phenomena.

Speaking in a general way, the delay of tidal epochs from point to point may be said to increase slowly as we go up the river, while the delay of the current epochs decreases rapidly.

Phenomena in the Pathway of the Hudson.

In Table No. 12 we have given the velocities of the currents at different depths below the surface, at our principal stations, in the pathway of the Hudson River; and in Diagram C. we have plotted the results for alternate lunar hours, so as to exhibit the changes from the Narrows to 41st-street.

You will observe, from this table (12) and Diagram C., that over the bar the greatest velocities near the bottom are reached during the ebb, but that at and above the Narrows the flood seems to predominate over the ebb *along the channel beds whenever the depth exceeds six fathoms.* In reports some years ago, I called your attention to the fact, that for several consecutive hours we had, at the mouth of the Hudson, a comparatively fresh stream running seaward upon the surface, and a salt stream taking the opposite course below. I conceived that in the months of summer, the season of our work, the head of the river so declines, that it cannot balance the seawater which consequently flows in along the bed. During the past two seasons, we have taken pains to measure densities, and have traced the sea water along the channel bed as high up as Carthage, 70 miles from Sandy Hook ; but the surface water was found essentially fresh at Teller's Point, 43 miles from Sandy Hook.

There is native oyster found in the Tappan Sea which is too small for the market, but is a favorite for planting in the Great South Bay of Long Island, where, with more sea water, it is said to grow to the ordinary size. It was reported to us that oysters had also been found in Haverstraw Bay, and sea crabs as high up as Carthage, ten miles below Poughkeepsie.

In Table No. 13 we give the specific gravities observed at the different stations, corrected for temperature by Halstrom's rule. These data were collected by Mr. Marindin, while our current observations were in progress in the year 1871. The water was pumped up through pipes, so that no mixtures of different strata affect our table.

The density of the sea on the chord of the great bay which lies between Nantucket and the capes of the Delaware was observed by me in 1867, and found to be 1.024 at temperature of 60°. This may be set down as the normal density of the Atlantic in the *approach* to our coast, while yet beyond the direct influence of our rivers. In the year 1865 we made some observations upon temperature and density between New-York and Cape Cod by the inland route, finding in the Race a density of 1.0224, and outside 1.0233, which density was carried through the Vineyard and Nantucket Sounds. Observations of 1871 in the Race gave us a density of 1.024.

It appears from our table (No. 13) that in the portion of the Hudson bordering on New-York City there is no great contrast of densities between the top and bottom of the sea, although it is decidedly marked at 20th-street at the close of the ebb current. Above this point there is a rapidly increasing variation of density with the depth for the close of the flood current; but the close of the ebb current presents little contrast of densities until we get above Dobb's Ferry or well into the Tappan Sea. At Teller's Point, which lies between the Tappan Sea and Haverstraw Bay, the differences of density between surface and bottom are very great. It would seem that these great basins store up the sea water, somewhat as does the Mystic Pond at the head of Mystic River above Boston. (See Special Report of U. S. Commissioners on Boston Harbor, published in 1861.)

The great basins terminate, essentially, at Verplanck's Point, where the difference between surface and deep water is conspicuous only on the flood. Above this point all contrast declines, and finally, at Barnegat, 75 miles from Sandy Hook, the river is of uniform density at all depths, being essentially fresh.

Although no critical comparison can be made between the different stations represented in Table No. 12, because the observations were not simultaneous, and have not been corrected for half-monthly inequalities; yet we may venture to suggest that at the depth of 22 feet at low water—which is that of the bar channel—there is still ample seaward scouring force all along the line; that the bar does not lie in the dead angle between the salt and fresh water, but, in its general character, belongs to the same class as those at our Southern inlets; in other words, it is a broken part of the *littoral cordon* of sand that skirts the coast, and is kept open in this case by the tidal circulation, which I have referred to in previous reports as the "*life blood of the harbor.*"

MOVEMENTS THROUGH THE EAST RIVER.

In Table No. 11 we have given the tidal elements of the East
River and its approaches. These elements are from actual observations, which we have not attempted to "adjust" as in the previous
tables. The currents of the East River, from the southern entrance
of Buttermilk Channel to Throg's Neck, belong to the *interference*
system, which I have discussed in my report on Hell Gate, Appendix
No. 13, of the Coast Survey Report, published separately in 1869.
I find it necessary to quote a few paragraphs from this report in
order to illustrate my subject, and explain in what manner this table
(No. 11) differs from those previously given for the Hudson :

"New-York Harbor is visited by two derivations from the tide-
" wave of the ocean, one of which approaches by way of Long
" Island Sound, the other by way of Sandy Hook entrance. These
" two tides meet and cross or overlap each other at Hell Gate ; and
" since they differ from each other in times and heights, they cause
" contrasts of water elevations between the Sound and the harbor,
" which call into existence the violent currents that traverse the
" East River.

" In the course of our laborious tabulations of the data from my
" physical surveys of 1857 and 1858, it has become apparent that
" the general order or scheme of the tidal interference is very sim-
" ple, and that the apparent complications result from the mingling
" of local peculiarities ; for this reason, I deem it essential to offer a
" general view of the scheme denuded of all its details, before in-
" viting you to follow through tables and diagrams to the phe-
" nomena actually observed.

" If the entrance from the Sound were closed at Throg's Neck,
" the tide which comes in over the bar would prevail all over New-
" York Harbor, and we should have on the west side of Hell Gate
" a tide of four and a half feet range, with its time of high water
" about one-half hour later than at Sandy Hook, i. e., eight and a
" half hours after the southing of the moon. In passing through
" the Gate and spreading out upon the broader spaces beyond, this
" tide would essentially lose its wave character, and become very
" much reduced in range, so that at the Brothers' Islands it would
" be scarcely sensible.

" If, on the other hand, the Sound entrance were to remain open
" and the Sandy Hook entrance be closed, a very different order of
" tides would prevail. On the east side of Hell Gate the tide would
" have a range of about seven feet, and high water would occur

"there about twelve hours after the moon's transit. In passing the
" Gate it would suffer degradation, but not very rapidly, till it had
" advanced beyond the Blackwell's Island channels. In the basin
" of the upper harbor, however, it would become very small, and
" essentially waste itself and disappear in the lower harbor. If
" these two suppositions are correct, we ought, with both entrances
" open, to find at Hell Gate a tide whose times and heights are in-
" termediate between those now observed at Sandy Hook on the
" one hand, and Throg's Neck upon the other; while at other points
" the proportions would be unequal, according as our place of ob-
" servation was more distant from the meeting point on either
" side."

     *   *   *   *   *   *   *   *   *   *   *

" Premising that *all currents are caused by disturbances of the
" surface level*, we may see, without effort, that in harbors visited
" by a single tide wave, (not materially distorted in its figure from
" point to point,) *slack current* must follow the *stand* of the tide,
" since at this time the surface level is restored. Again, for this
" single tide, the maximum velocity must occur near the time of
" half tide, because at this time the greatest rise or fall, and, con-
" sequently, the greatest filling or draining, is taking place. In the
" neighborhood of Sandy Hook or at Throg's Neck, the currents
" do follow in the manner we have stated, the local tide; but in the
" East River, where two tide waves approach from opposite direc-
" tions, the changes of surface level, and consequently the currents,
" bear no direct relation to either tide wave considered by itself,
" but depend upon the nature of the "interference," as it is called.

     *   *   *   *   *   *   *   *

" These differences of surface level are the vertical measures of
" the slopes—tidal *heads*, if we may use this term so loosely-- and
" they increase from zero to maximum (4.87 feet) in about three
" hours, then decline to zero in about the same time.

     *   *   *   *   *   *   *   *

" The following summary of the leading points which I have
" attempted to illustrate, will serve as my guide in the arrangement
" of my observed data :

" *First.* Two tide waves visit New-York Harbor, meeting and
" overlapping at Hell Gate.

" *Second.* Near the meeting point of these two tides the observed
" heights and times of the compound tide are intermediate.

" *Third.* The currents of Hell Gate are called into existence by
" the variations in the relative heights of the Sound and harbor;
" their epochs have no direct relations with those of the local tide
" or its components, and their velocities do not depend upon the
" local rates of rise or fall of tide.

" *Fourth.* The current flowing westward through Hell Gate
" occupies a greater section than that flowing to the eastward,
" because the former prevails during higher stages of the local tide
" than the latter."

The third point made in the above quotation seems to be con-
firmed, because we find that subtracting the observed tides on the
east side of the Gate from those observed upon the west side, we
have maximum differences of level at 6h. 41m. and 12h. 13m. after
the transit, and the maximum velocity of the tidal currents at the
north end of Blackwell's Island, (see Table 11,) at 6h. 30m. and
12h. 38m. When we consider that these differences of level and
times of maximum velocity are modified by so many local circum-
stances, the reaction of numerous reefs, the passing of great fleets
of vessels, the winds, &c., I think the above agreements are about
as near as we could expect from short series. If we had observed
long series of tides at Throg's Neck and Governor's Island, which
we did not, I have no doubt we should have come much closer.
Mr. STRIEDINGER, an assistant to Maj. Gen. NEWTON, who has
leveled very closely through the Gate, tells me that the local disturbances are very considerable as reflected in the varying slopes.
We may, without material error, use the following rule for the
East River current :

*The strength of the flood current occurs six hours and a half after
the transit of the moon, and the strength of the ebb current at twelve
hours and a half after the same transit,* (or about twenty minutes
after the immediately preceding transit.)

The above rule at neap tides will cover the axis of the entire
channel from Atlantic Dock to Throg's Neck, but at spring tides
would extend easterly only as far as Old Ferry Point.

Current observations at the Race were made, but under circum-
stances not altogether favorable, and those for points below the
surface I have rejected as far as velocities are concerned, because I
am convinced that the stray line (whose outrun is designed to per-

mit the lower log to sink to the full length of the connecting wire, before the observer begins to count) was not in this case long enough, so that added to the real velocity is the descent of the log in part. Our vessel was anchored in 40 fathoms of water. Concerning the tides and currents of Long Island Sound, Mr. Schott has written a paper in the Coast Survey Report of 1854.

In Table No. 14 we furnish the observations made at several stations simultaneously in a line across the East River at Wallstreet. The velocities given are those observed at the surface, but a pretty thorough examination was made of those below the surface, without revealing any changes which we could connect with the lunar hours.

By reason of the delay of the tide through the East River, the relations of flowage to section differ from point to point. While at Hell Gate the greater section is that of ebb, (westerly flow,) the greater section at Wall-street occurs during the flood, (easterly flow.) You will learn from Table No. 15, which is made out from very careful data—comprising velocities at different depths, at different distances across the stream and at different times—that the section during the flood is 91,560 against 86,960 square feet during the ebb. The volumes passing in the two directions are much the same. The small difference which appears in the table is probably due to errors in reduction. The mean movement is that of 4,362,300,000 cubic feet in either direction. If a canal of the same width and section as the East River at this point were extended without limit and visited like the Hudson, by one tide only, no such movement as this could be generated—this is a matter of computation—so that the phenomena we have observed are those peculiar to the co-existence of *two inlets* traversed by *different tides*. The strong currents in the pass between Martha's Vineyard and the main land in the neighborhood of Vineyard Haven, where the channel is over three miles wide and more than 60 feet deep in the average, are due entirely to the *interference* of two tides differing, like those that visit New-York harbor, both in time and range.

EAST RIVER AND HUDSON TIDAL CURRENTS COMPARED.

Table No. 16 gives in detail the soundings and positions of stations, in two cross sections, one of which was in the East River, and has been commented upon, the other in the North River, at 42d-street.

Table No. 17 contains our observations at 42d-street, in full, together with a recapitulation of the velocities, arranged according to lunar hours, and corresponding to Table No. 14. These observations are illustrated upon Diagram D., in explanation of which I shall offer a few comments. The curves are those for surface velocities, and do not represent the movements for all depths. Those above the axis are plotted from flood velocities, which take a northwardly direction in the Hudson and an easterly direction in the East River, while those below the axis are reverse courses. In the first figure of this diagram the abscissas are hours of civil time, but in all the others they measure distances from the west shore. In Fig. 1st it will be observed that the ebb is everywhere in excess of the flood, but most conspicuously so in the middle of the river, and least so upon the western shore where the two drifts approach equality. These curves indicate that *middle time* as well as all other elements vary in the transverse section, and that some of the irregularities which appear in Tables 9 and 10 are due to the circumstance that our stations were not always located in the axis of the stream.

Passing on to the transverse curves you will observe that for nearly three hours, between III. and VI. hours after the transit, the ebb of the Hudson may be supposed in part to flow towards the Sound; while the East River ebb is a tributary of the Hudson flood for scarcely two hours, between IX. and XI. hours. You will bear in mind that the terms "flood" and "ebb," as applied to the East River streams, are merely used in their popular sense. The general inference from the above statements would be that the East River is an outlet and feeder of the Hudson for several hours of each day.

RELATIONS OF EAST RIVER MOVEMENTS TO THOSE OVER THE BAR.

Computations made upon the observations at different depths, in 1858, gave for the discharge of the Hudson, at the close of the wet season, (June 1st,) 6,038 millions of cubic feet, and at the close of the dry season, (September,) 3,360 millions. Our more extended observations of 1872 (October) gave nearly equal inflows and outflows, amounting to 4,511 millions, which is about the mean of the two gaugings of 1858. Now this added to the ebb volume of the East River, which was 4,383 millions, give 8,894 millions. If to this we add the harbor tidal prism, 17,862 millions, (which includes Newark and Raritan Bays and the Kills,) we have 26,756 millions of cubic feet. The gauging across the mouth of the harbor, from Sandy Hook to Coney Island, gave, from observations of 1858, an outflow of 27,663 millions of cubic feet, which is only about two and a half per cent. more than the preceding computation. Perhaps this little excess is due to the discharges of streams and creeks, not considered in the previous computation because not gauged. I confess that I had expected a much greater excess, because I had not counted in the Passaic, Hackensack, Raritan and Shrewsbury rivers, from which considerable volumes, even in the dry season, must escape by way of Sandy Hook and by way of Hell Gate. Without claiming that *all* the water that comes in through the East River goes out over the bar and aids in the scour of its channel, I think this computation authorizes us to regard the East River stream as too important to be treated lightly.

I think you have fully explained the entire discrepancy between the views expressed by Mr. Dow and those which we have based upon our observations, in pointing out that Mr. Dow is reasoning upon the supposition of a harbor visited by a single tide entering ·simultaneously by two mouths.* If this supposition were correct, *i. e.*, if the same tidal undulation came up from Throg's Neck and in over the bar at the same time, the office of draining and filling the harbor and river with tide water would be divided between the two outlets, and the currents of the flood and ebb would be much weaker than now through these outlets,—much weaker, in such a case, with two outlets than with one, of course. But as a matter of fact the order of things is quite different from these supposed cases. The tide coming in at Sandy Hook not only has to feed New-York Harbor but for a while the Sound also ; and *vice versa*, the water flowing in from the East River not only has to feed the harbor and its rivers, but the ocean outside of Sandy Hook (being for several hours at a lower level than the East River) receives the drainage of the Sound in addition to that of the harbor. In this way New-York bar is crossed in either direction by a volume of water much greater than the simple filling and emptying of New-York Harbor and its rivers would demand. If you were to close the East River by a dam, you would reduce both flood and ebb currents on the bar very sensibly, because, as we have seen, several millions of cubic feet would be cut off which now traverse the seaward channels four times a day.

I must add one general statement concerning a harbor with two or more outlets. It does not follow, even when such a harbor is visited by only one tide, that there is a disadvantage in having more

---

* Excuse me. This was not my supposition. I well knew the difference of time in the Sandy Hook and Hell Gate tides.—G. W. Dow.

than one pathway to the sea. On the contrary, a majority of the first class harbors of the world have several. Among sands, it is not wholly upon the strength of the current that *effective* scour depends, but upon the power of these to dispose of the material advantageously. Equal and opposite tidal currents, however strong, cannot remove the bars of our southern inlets, because, in the short period of six hours, the very slow *dune-like* movement of the sand has not carried it beyond the influence of the adverse stream with which it works back to its old place; but where the ebb and flood are unequal, the material is swept entirely away from the mouth of the harbor. Now, with harbors of two outlets, it often happens (and I speak here with plenty of observed data at my command) that one channel is more favorably situated for discharge than the other, so that, in *effect*, there is a circulation, *in at one door and out at the other.* It is precisely for the sake of inducing such a circulation, that a second outlet is now being constructed from a sandy harbor on the west coast of Denmark.

One may presume, that if there were no tides at all in New-York, the two openings would still be of advantage to each other. In a northeast gale, for instance, the Sound waters, driven before the wind, mount up several feet at Hell Gate, and would rise much higher, except that they escape through the harbor of New-York, and out to sea over the bar. In this case, the entire Sound is useful, because it is a shallow sea, in which the effect of the wind is largely *translation,* instead of *oscillation,* (as in the ocean.) The wind cannot blow from any quarter without disturbing the balance of the two outlets, and this disturbance is represented in effective scour at the bar.

Very respectfully, yours,

HENRY MITCHELL.

Prof. BENJAMIN PEIRCE,
Superintendent U. S. Coast Survey.

LIST OF TABLES AND DIAGRAMS ACCOMPANYING REPORT

OF PROF. HENRY MITCHELL.

————•♦•————

TABLES.

CHANGES ON THE JERSEY FLATS.

No. 1.—Advance or Retreat of the Border of the Flats between Robbins' Reef Light and Central R. R. Wharf.
No. 2.—Increase or Decrease of the Point of the Flats.
No. 3.—Increase or Decrease of Horizontal Areas.
No. 4.—Increase or Decrease of Volumes.

CHANGES IN THE VICINITY OF GOWANUS BAY.

No. 5.—Depth of Water in 1855.
No. 6.—   do.   do.   1872.
No. 7.—Changes of Depth between 1855 and 1872.

No. 8.—Currents of Gedney's Channel.
No. 9.—Tides and Currents in Hudson River and approaches.
No. 10.—Tidal Elements of Hudson River adjusted.
No. 11.—Tides and Currents in East River and approaches.
No. 12.—Currents at different Depths.
No. 13.—Specific Gravities of Water in the Hudson River.
No. 14.—Currents of East River at Wall Street.
No. 15.—Volumes passing through East River at Wall Street.
No. 16.—Mean Low Water Sections at 42d Street and Wall Street.
No. 17.—Currents of Hudson River off 42d Street.

~~~~~~~~~~~~~~~

DIAGRAMS.

A.—Showing method of computing Changes on Jersey Flats.
B.—Showing Changes in the vicinity of Gowanus Bay.
C.—Showing vertical Current Curves, also method of computing "Middle Time."
D.—Transverse Curves of Velocities in Hudson and East Rivers.

Table No. 1.

Changes on the Jersey Flats, New-York Harbor, as shown by the Surveys of 1855 and 1871–72.

No. of Normal from Robbins' Reef Light.	Distances from the Datum Line of the 6, 12, 18, 24 and 30 Feet Curves. 6 Feet Curve. 1855.	6 Feet Curve. 1871–72.	6 Feet Curve. Advance (+) or Retreat (—.)	12 Feet Curve. 1855.	12 Feet Curve. 1871–72.	12 Feet Curve. Advance (+) or Retreat (—.)	18 Feet Curve. 1855.	18 Feet Curve. 1871–72.	18 Feet Curve. Advance (+) or Retreat (—.)	24 Feet Curve. 1855.	24 Feet Curve. 1871–72.	24 Feet Curve. Advance (+) or Retreat (—.)	30 Feet Curve. 1855.	30 Feet Curve. 1871–72.	30 Feet Curve. Advance (+) or Retreat (—.)	Depths on the Datum Line. 1855.	Depths on the Datum Line. 1871–72.	Depths on the Datum Line. Diff.
	Feet.	Feet.	Feet.	Feet.	Feet.	Feet.	Feet.	Feet.	Feet.	Feet.	Feet.	Feet.	Feet.	Feet.	Feet.	Feet.	Feet.	Feet.
0....	....	....	....	495	630	+135	825	905	+80	930	1,065	+135	1,160	1,165	+5	0	0	0
I....	....	....	....	290	515	+225	570	850	+280	650	970	+320	1,115	1,075	—40	8½	8	—½
II....	....	....	....	175	335	+160	380	750	+370	565	860	+295	975	1,020	+45	10	9½	—½
III....	....	....	....	90	165	+75	275	620	+345	550	850	+300	850	935	+85	10	10½	+½
IV....	....	....	....	0	40	+40	200	285	+85	410	700	+290	800	900	+100	12	11½	—½
V....	....	....	....	....	....	....	150	210	+60	460	570	+110	775	900	+125	14	13	—1
VI....	....	....	....	....	....	....	100	170	+70	400	575	+175	825	825	0	15	13	—2
VII....	....	....	....	....	....	....	60	175	+115	315	575	+260	820	740	—80	16	14½	—1½
VIII....	....	...	....	....	....	....	0	225	+225	250	525	+275	825	740	—85	18	15	—3
IX....	....	....	....	....	....	....	0	285	+285	200	500	+290	760	725	—35	18	15½	—2½
X....	....	....	....	....	....	....	0	320	+320	185	500	+315	730	765	+35	18	16	—2
XI....	....	....	....	....	....	....	0	325	+325	150	500	+350	700	785	—85	18	15	—3
XII....	....	....	....	....	....	....	15	225	+210	190	515	+325	625	810	+185	17	14	—3
XIII....	...	....	....	....	....	....	50	125	+75	185	600	+415	590	835	+245	16	14	—2
XIV....	....	....	....	...	....	....	60	110	+50	175	625	+450	575	875	+300	17½	14½	—3
XV....	....	....	....	....	0	0	70	225	+155	275	800	+525	575	950	+375	16	12	—4
XVI....	....	....	....	....	350	+350	110	820	+710	320	1,050	+730	585	1,220	+635	16	9½	—6½
XVII....	....	....	....	40	1,075	+1,035	215	1,145	+930	450	1,275	+825	590	1,375	+785	10	9½	—½
XVIII....	....	....	....	130	800	+670	265	975	+710	490	1,190	+700	640	1,320	+680	6¾	7½	+¾
XIX....	40	....	—40	235	440	+205	330	675	+345	550	985	+435	660	1,180	+520	5	6½	+1½
XX....	160	120	—40	310	280	—30	465	400	—65	575	875	+300	690	1,185	+495	4	3	—1
XXI....	135	210	+75	325	285	—40	445	500	+55	625	850	+225	725	1,150	+425	5	3	—2
XXII....	65	110	+45	355	325	—30	475	440	—35	610	880	+270	775	1,160	+385	5½	5½	0
XXIII....	80	135	+55	375	330	—45	530	525	—5	650	965	+315	860	1,270	+410	5	3½	—1½
XXIV....	230	230	0	400	360	—40	475	900	+425	735	1,285	+550	950	1,400	+450	5½	4½	—1
XXV....	330	360	+30	420	365	—55	480	575	+95	750	1,175	+425	985	1,400	+415	5½	3½	—2
XXVI....	375	345	—30	465	410	—55	575	430	—145	825	1,200	+375	1,075	1,425	+350	0	0	0
XXVII....	370	370	0	635	575	—60	840	1,120	+280	1,180	1,375	+195	1,350	1,500	+150	3	3	0
XXVIII....	340	365	+25	790	675	—115	1,115	1,160	+45	1,210	1,515	+305	1,430	1,635	+205	3	3¾	+¾
XXIX....	375	400	+25	900	725	—175	1,200	1,270	+70	1,450	1,580	+130	1,570	1,770	+200	5	4½	—½
XXX....	415	460	+45	915	765	—150	1,175	1,290	+115	1,375	1,650	+275	1,625	1,870	+245	5	5	0
XXXI....	450	450	0	840	780	—60	1,020	1,230	+210	1,150	1,700	+550	1,720	1,910	+190	5	4½	—½
XXXII....	500	430	—70	750	710	—40	875	1,270	+395	1,525	1,710	+185	1,920	2,025	+105	4½	4½	0
XXXIII....	550	487	—63	710	645	—65	835	1,285	+450	1,475	1,725	+250	2,100	2,080	—20	4½	4½	0
XXXIV....	470	525	+55	685	800	+115	790	1,280	+490	1,700	1,650	—50	2,175	2,115	—60	0	0	0
XXXV....	265	550	+285	640	875	+235	1,360	1,250	—110	1,635	1,590	—45	2,240	2,125	—115	3	3	0
XXXVI....	75	565	+490	540	880	+340	1,175	1,240	+65	1,610	1,690	+80	2,230	2,165	—65	4	4½	+½
XXXVII....	....	540	+540	425	550	+125	1,050	1,100	+50	1,550	1,470	—80	2,140	2,075	—65	6	4½	—1½
XXXVIII....	....	....	....	360	290	—70	950	920	—30	1,610	1,415	—195	1,910	1,920	+10	7	10	+3
Mean.			+54			+106			+211			+303			+201			

Note.—The normals, which are 500 feet apart, are drawn towards the channel from a datum line, which runs through Robbins' Reef Light House to Bedloe's Island Flagstaff, thence, deflecting slightly through Ellis' Island Flagstaff to the New-Jersey Central Rail-Road Wharf.

ED. H. FOOTE, *Computer*.

Table No. 2.

CHANGES ON THE POINT OF JERSEY FLATS, NEW-YORK HARBOR, AS SHOWN BY THE SURVEYS OF 1855 AND 1871-72.

DISTANCES FROM ROBBINS' REEF LIGHT (ON RADII FROM THE LIGHT) OF THE 6, 12, 18, 24 AND 30 FEET CURVES.

No. of Radius.	6 feet Curve.			12 feet Curve.			18 feet Curve.			24 feet Curve.			30 feet Curve.		
	1855.	1871-72.	Advance (+) or Retreat (—).	1855.	1871-72.	Advance (+) or Retreat (—).	1855.	1871-72.	Advance (+) or Retreat (—).	1855.	1871-72.	Advance (+) or Retreat (—).	1855.	1871-72.	Advance (+) or Retreat (—).
	Feet.	Feet.	Feet.	Feet.	Feet.	Feet.	Feet.	Feet.	Feet.	Feet.	Feet.	Feet.	Feet.	Feet.	Feet.
0........	130	210	+ 60	495	630	+135	825	905	+ 80	930	1,065	+135	1,100	1,165	+ 5
I........	210	200	— 40	635	750	+115	1,110	970	—140	1,200	1,150	— 50	1,330	1,280	— 50
II........	325	165	—160	925	925	0	1,395	1,180	—215	1,310	1,490	— 50	1,875	1,675	—200
III........	375	175	—200	1,030	995	— 35	1,615	1,555	— 60	2,030	1,970	— 60	2,500	2,250	—250
IV........	400	190	—210	1,010	970	— 70	1,610	1,470	—170	1,980	2,050	+ 70	2,800	2,730	— 70
Mean....	...	...	—118	...	...	+ 28	...	...	—115	...	...	— 11	...	...	—133

NOTE.—The radii are drawn 22° 30′ apart, from Robbins' Reef Light as a centre, No. 0 being perpendicular to a line from the Light House to Bedloe's Island Flagstaff.

ED. H. FOOTE, *Computer.*

Table No. 3.

CHANGES ON THE JERSEY FLATS, NEW-YORK HARBOR, AS SHOWN BY THE SURVEYS OF 1855 AND 1871–72.

BETWEEN NORMALS.	INCREASE OR DECREASE OF HORIZONTAL AREA.				
	6 ft. Plane.	12 ft. Plane.	18 ft. Plane.	24 ft. Plane.	30 ft. Plane.
	Sq. ft.	*Sq. ft.*	*Sq. ft.*	*Sq. ft.*	*Sq. ft.*
0 and II	....	+ 186,250	+ 252,500	+ 267,500	− 7,500
II. and IV	....	+ 87,500	+ 236,250	+ 296,250	+ 78,500
IV. and VI	....	....	+ 63,750	+ 171,250	+ 87,500
VI. and VIII	....	....	+ 131,250	+ 242,500	− 61,250
VIII. and X	....	....	+ 278,750	+ 287,500	− 30,000
X. and XII	....	....	+ 295,000	+ 335,000	+ 97,500
XII. and XIV	....	....	+ 102,500	+ 401,250	+ 243,750
XIV. and XVI	....	....	+ 267,500	+ 557,500	+ 421,250
XVI. and XVIII	....	+ 772,500	+ 820,000	+ 770,000	+ 716,250
XVIII. and XX	....	+ 162,500	+ 333,750	+ 467,500	+ 548,750
XX. and XXII	+ 38,750	− 40,000	+ 2,500	+ 255,000	+ 432,500
XXII. and XXIV	+ 38,750	− 25,000	+ 95,000	+ 362,500	+ 413,750
XXIV. and XXVI	+ 7,500	− 46,250	+ 117,600	+ 443,750	+ 407,500
XXVI. and XXVIII	− 1,250	− 80,000	+ 165,000	+ 267,500	+ 213,750
XXVIII. and XXX	+ 30,000	− 161,250	+ 75,000	+ 142,500	+ 212,500
XXX. and XXXII	− 6,250	− 77,500	+ 247,500	+ 322,500	+ 187,500
XXXII. and XXXIV	− 35,250	− 8,750	+ 446,250	+ 158,750	+ 1,250
XXXIV. and XXXVI	+278,750	+ 236,750	+ 83,750	− 30,000	− 88,750
XXXVI. and XXXVIII	....	+ 280,000	+ 33,750	− 83,750	− 46,250
Total,	+351,000	+1,286,750	+4,052,500	+5,635,000	+3,828,500

Table No. 4.

CHANGES ON THE JERSEY FLATS, NEW-YORK HARBOR, AS SHOWN BY THE SURVEYS OF 1855 AND 1871-72.

BETWEEN NORMALS.	INCREASE OR DECREASE OF VOLUME BETWEEN					TOTAL.
	Datum line & 6 ft.	6 ft. & 12 ft.	12 ft. & 19 ft.	18 ft. & 24 ft.	21 ft. & 30 ft.	
	Cu. ft.	Cu. ft.	Cu. ft.	Cu. ft.	Cu. ft.	Cu. ft.
0 and II.........	....	+ 525,000*	+ 1,316,250	+ 1,556,500	+ 765,000	+ 4,162,750
II. and IV........	....	+ 82,000*	+ 971,250	+ 1,597,500	+ 1,125,000	+ 3,775,750
IV. and VI.......	....	....	+ 270,000	+ 720,000	+ 776,250	+ 1,776,250
VI. and VIII......	....	....	+ 271,250	+ 1,121,250	+ 543,750	+ 1,936,250
VIII. and X.........	....	....	+ 342,500	+ 1,698,750	+ 772,500	+ 2,813,750
X. and XII.......	....	....	+ 434,000	+ 1,887,500	+ 1,207,500	+ 3,619,000
XII. and XIV......	....	....	+ 267,250	+ 1,511,250	+ 1,435,000	+ 3,213,500
XIV. and XVI......	....	....	+ 1,196,750	+ 2,475,000	+ 1,936,250	+ 5,608,000
XVI. and XVIII....	...	+ 1,078,000*	+ 4,836,250	+ 4,770,000	+ 3,458,750	+ 14,143,000
XVIII. and XX.......	....	+ 542,000	+ 1,777,500	+ 2,403,750	+ 3,051,250	+ 7,774,500
XX. and XXII.....	+ 132,000	— 3,500	— 112,500	+ 772,500	+ 2,062,500	+ 2,851,000
XXII. and XXIV.....	+ 96,000	+ 41,250	+ 460,000	+ 1,372,500	+ 2,328,750	+ 4,298,500
XXIV. and XXVI.....	+ 190,000	— 116,250	+ 463,750	+ 1,683,750	+ 2,553,750	+ 4,775,000
XXVI. and XXVIII..	— 48,000	— 251,250	+ 105,000	+ 1,147,500	+ 1,443,750	+ 2,397,000
XXVIII. and XXX......	+ 40,000	— 393,750	— 258,750	+ 885,000	+ 1,267,500	+ 1,540,000
XXX. and XXXII....	+ 48,000	— 251,250	+ 510,000	+ 1,912,500	+ 1,717,500	+ 3,936,750
XXXII. and XXXIV...	+ 3,000	— 132,000	+ 1,312,500	+ 1,815,000	+ 480,000	+ 3,478,500
XXXIV. and XXXVI...	+ 341,000	+ 1,545,000	+ 960,000	+ 161,250	— 356,250	+ 2,651,000
XXXVI. and XXXVIII.	....	+ 1,917,500	+ 941,250	— 150,000	— 390,000	+ 2,318,750
Total,.............	+ 802,000	+ 4,582,750	+ 16,064,250	+ 29,141,500	+ 26,268,750	+ 76,859,250

REMARKS.—Volumes marked with a star (*) are between the datum line and the 12 ft. line.

Table No. 5.

CHANGES IN THE BOTTOM OF NEW-YORK HARBOR IN THE VICINITY OF THE MIDDLE GROUND SHOAL. FROM A COMPARISON OF THE SURVEYS OF 1835 AND 1872.

DEPTHS AT THE NERVALS AT POINTS 100 FEET APART EACH WAY FROM THE AXIS, IN 1835.

CHANGES IN THE BOTTOM OF NEW-YORK HARBOR IN THE VICINITY OF THE MIDDLE GROUND SHOAL. FROM A COMPARISON OF THE SURVEYS OF 1835 AND 1873.

DEPTHS OF THE SOUNDINGS, AT POINTS 250 FEET APART EACH WAY FROM THE AXIS, IN 1873.

| No. of Ranges from Bay Ridge Flagstaff | | | | | | Distances from the Axis towards the Main Channel. | | | | | | | | | | | | | | | | | | | | Axis | | Distances from the Axis towards the Shore. | | | | | | | | | | | | | | | | | | | | |

CHANGES IN THE BOTTOM OF NEW YORK HARBOR IN THE VICINITY OF THE MIDDLE GROUND SHOAL. FROM A COMPARISON OF THE SURVEYS OF 1855 AND 1878.

ED. E. FOOTE, Computer.

Table No. 8.

CURRENTS OF GEDNEY'S CHANNEL.

1858.

Time.	Velocity.	Time.	Velocity.	Time.	Velocity.	REMARKS.
Aug. 7.	Naut. miles.	Aug. 8.	Naut. miles.	Aug. 8.	Naut. miles.	A diagram accompanies this table. Between the hours of 10 and 13, on the 8th, some irregularities of the observed curve are swept out by a graphical correction.
h. m.		h. m.		h. m.		
13 00	—0.05	1 00	—0.80	13 00	—1.00	
13 30	+0.40	1 30	—0.40	13 30	—0.45	
14 00	+1.00	2 00	+0.15	14 00	—0.20	
14 30	+1.20	2 30	+0.40			
15 00	+1.35	3 00	+0.75			
15 30	+1.45	3 30	+1.00			
16 00	+1.52	4 00	+1.15			
16 30	+1.42	4 30	+1.25			
17 00	+1.32	5 00	+1.25			
17 30	+1.20	5 30	+1.20			
18 00	+1.07	6 00	+0.90			
18 30	+0.80	6 30	+0.70			
19 00	+0.57	7 00	+0.35			
19 30	—0.10	7 30	+0.07			
20 00	—0.75	8 00	—0.20			
20 30	—1.00	8 30	—0.65			
21 00	—1.45	9 00	—1.20			
21 30	—1.85	9 30	—1.65		•	
22 00	—2.15	10 00	—1.98			
22 30	—1.80	10 30	—2.00			
23 00	—1.65	11 00	—1.87			
23 30	—1.48	11 30	—1.70			
Aug. 8.						
h. m.						
0 00	—1.40	12 00	—1.47			
0 30	—1.05	12 30	—1.22			

ED. H. FOOTE, *Computer*.

Table No. 9.

Tides and Currents Observed in the Hudson River and Seaward Approaches.

Localities.	Flood Current. Middle Time after Transit.	Flood Current. Direction.	Flood Current. Max. Velocity.	Flood Current. No. of Determinations.	Ebb Current. Middle Time after Transit.	Ebb Current. Directions.	Ebb Current. Max. Velocity.	Ebb Current. No. of Determinations.	Tides. Intervals. H. W. h.	Tides. Intervals. H. W. m.	Tides. Intervals. L. W. h.	Tides. Intervals. L. W. m.	Tides. Rise and Fall.	Distance from Sandy Hook.	
	h. m.		Naut. Miles.		h. m.		Naut. Miles.		h.	m.	h.	m.	Feet.	Naut. Miles.	
40 miles S. of Fire Id. Lt.,	1 41	S. W.	0.70	1	8 16	E.	0.33	1	....		....		....	—60	Feeble and irregular.
Sandy Hook Lt. Ship,....	5 18	N. W.	0.57	4	12 38	S. E.	0.45	2	....		....		....	— 6¾	
Sta. J. Gedney's Channel,	5 30	W.	1.45	2	11 38	E.	2.07	2	....		....		....	— 3	
Sandy Hook,............	....	....	....	..	....	....	....	..	VII.	XXIX.	XIII.	XLIV.	4.8	0	
Main Ch. (bet. E. & W. Banks,).........	7 03	N.	1.40	25	13 03	S.	2.10	23	....		....		....	5¼	
Narrows,................	6 57	N. W.	1.10	8	13 10	S. E.	1.60	7	....		....		....	7⅛	
Main Ch. (bet. Gov. and Bedloe's Islands,.......	7 54	N.	0.91	..	14 04	S.	1.70	..	VIII.	XIII.	XIV.	XXXVIII.	4.4	13 1-6	
Off 42d-st., Hudson R.	8 55	"	1.47	..	14 55	"	2.78	..	....		....		....	18⅝	
" 96th-st., "	8 37	"	1.17	1	15 01	"	1.85	2	....		....		....	20⅝	
" Dobbs' Ferry, "	9 32	"	1.35	1	16 23	"	1.25	1	IX.	VIII.	XVI.	XXXVII.	3.6	31¼	
" Tarrytown, "	10 12	"	1.00	1	15 51	"	0.75	1	....		....		3.5	38⅛	
" Teller's Pt., "	....	..	....	..	17 42	"	0.70	2	....		....		....	43½	
" Verplanck's Pt., "	....	..	....	..	16 50	"	0.70	2	X.	LIII.	XVIII.	V.	3.1	49½	
" Iona Id., "	....	..	....	..	17 03	"	1.10	1	....		....		....	53¼	
" Denning's Land'g, "	10 37	"	0.60	1	17 03	"	1.60	2	....		....		....	56¾	
" West Point, "	....	..	....	..	....	....	....	..	XI.	L.	XIX.	VI.	....	59½	
" Cold Spring, "	10 39	"	0.92	1	17 13	"	1.40	1	....		....		2.7	61	
" New Windsor, "	10 48	"	1.10	3	....	"	1.40	1	....		....		....	65	
" Carthage, "	11 05	"	1.30	2	....	"	1.20	2	....		....		....	70¼	
" Barnegat, "	11 11	"	1.20	2	....	"	1.40	1	....		....		....	75	
" Poughkeepsie, "	11 06	"	0.90	1	....	....	....	..	XIII.	XXXIX.	XX.	LIV.	3.2	79¼	

Table No. 10.

TIDAL ELEMENTS OF HUDSON RIVER ADJUSTED.

Distance from Sandy Hook	FLOOD Middle Time after Transit	FLOOD Dir.	EBB Middle Time after Transit	EBB Dir.	TIDES Intervals H.W.	TIDES Intervals L.W.	Rise and Fall	Mean Depth of Channel	Square Root of ½ Depth	Mean Depth at ½ Tide for entire Width	Mean Width	Mean Section	Mean Perimeter	Mean Radius	Change of Course Max.	Change of Course Sum.	GENERAL LOCALITY
Naut. miles.	*h. m.*		*h. m.*		*h. m.*	*h. m.*	*Feet.*	*Feet.*	*Feet.*	*Feet.*	*Feet.*	*Sq. Feet.*	*Feet.*	*Feet.*			
0	6 02	W'd.	12 18	E'd.	0 0	0 0	4.8	32	5.1	...	...	...	...	...	...	...	Sandy Hook.
10	7 33	N'd.	13 32	S'd.	0 XXIV.	0 XXIV.	4.4	59	5.4	...	...	...	...	...	...	...	Quarantine. New-York Bay. 86th Street.
20	8 42	::	15 03	::	0 LIX.	L VIII.	4.2	52	5.1	23	4,870	112,000	4,925	22.74	10°	10°	Yonkers. Tappan Sea.
30	9 27	::	15 57	::	I XXXIII.	I XXXIX.	3.9	43	4.6	16	8,860	139,000	8,894	15.63	15°	15°	Sleepy Hollow. Haverstraw Bay.
40	10 05	::	16 35	::	II IX.	II XXVI.	3.5	42	4.6	16	10,570	177,000	11,133	15.90	50°	89°	Verplanck's Point.
50	10 33	::	17 00	::	II XL.	III XXVII.	3.1	106	7.3	41	2,740	121,000	2,883	41.82	73°	288°	Highlands.
60	10 50	::	17 00	::	III XXX.	IV XXII.	2.8	60	5.5	25	5,080	131,000	5,125	26.14	40°	87°	Carthage.
70	11 01	::	...	::	IV XXVI.	V VII.	3.0	89	5.8	34	3,140	120,000	3,290	37.27	33°	81°	Poughkeepsie.
80	11 12	::	...	::	V XXVI.	V LVI.	3.2	...	...	...	...	...	...	...	...	...	

NOTE.—In plotting the courses we have drawn the longest possible lines within the Channel bounded by the 18 feet curves, each line beginning and ending in the middle of the Channel as thus bounded.

ED. H. FOOTE, *Computer.*

Table No. 11.

TIDES AND CURRENTS OBSERVED IN THE EAST RIVER AND APPROACHES.

Localities	Flood Current Middle Time after Transit (h. m.)	Flood Azim.	Flood Max. Velocity (Naut. Miles)	Flood No. of Determinations	Ebb Current Middle Time after Transit (h. m.)	Ebb Azim.	Ebb Max. Velocity (Naut. Miles)	Ebb No. of Determinations	Tides Intervals H.W. (h. m.)	Tides Intervals L.W. (h. m.)	Rise and Fall	Distance from Sandy Hook
Main Channel (off Sandy Hook.)	5 00	70°	2.03	3	11 15	274°	2.17	2	VII. XXIX.	...	...	1-5
Narrows	6 57	148°	1.10	8	13 10	330°	1.60	7	VIII. XIII.	XIV. XXIX.	4.24	5¾
Buttermilk Channel	6 33	N'd.	1.43	...	12 38	S'd.	1.77	...	...	...	...	12
East of Wall St. Ferry	6 33	"	...	...	12 28	"	...	...	...	...	...	14½
S. end of Blackwell's Island Channels	6 32	"	2 40	...	12 40	"	2.90	...	...	...	...	18¾
N. end of Blackwell's Island channels	6 30	E'd.	4 20	...	12 38	W'd.	4.20	...	X. VI.	XVI.	4.45	20
Hallet's Point	...	"	8 50	...	...	"	4.4	...	XII. VII.	XVII. LVIII.	5.68	20¾
Pot Cove	...	"	...	...	...	"	...	...	XII. XXIX.	XIX.	...	20¼
Polhemus' Dock to Lawrence Point	7 06	"	3 10	...	13 12	"	2.30	...	XI. XX.	XX.	...	22
Throg's Neck	6 33	"	0.75	...	12 43	"	0.70	...	...	...	...	26¼
Execution Rocks	4 15	"	1.50	...	10 25	"	0.80	...	...	...	...	32
Middle of Sound	4 08	"	0.60	...	10 18	"	0.50	...	...	...	...	...
Race	3 00* ... 2 01	"	...	...	9 06	"	...	...	IX. XXXVIII.	XXXVIII.	...	110½

Neaps.   Springs.

* This figure is computed from Mr. SCHOTT's Table, page 170 of Annual Report of Coast Survey for 1854.

Table No. 12.

CURRENTS AT DIFFERENT DEPTHS IN THE HUDSON RIVER AND NEW-YORK HARBOR. FROM OBSERVATIONS OF 1858 AND 1859.

LUNAR HOURS.	STATION IN GEDNEY'S CHANNEL. August 7th, 1858.						STATION IN MAIN SHIP CHANNEL OFF SANDY HOOK. August 8, 9, 10, 1858.						REMARKS.
	Velocity at Surface.	Dir.	Velocity at 11½ Feet.	Dir.	Velocity at 26½ Feet.	Dir.	Velocity at Surface.	Dir.	Velocity at 11½ Feet.	Dir.	Velocity at 40 Feet.	Dir.	
0	1.69	E'd	1.79	E'd	1.53	E'd	2.13	E'd	2.38	E'd	1.01	E'd	A diagram "C," accompanies this Table.
I	1.26	"	1.32	"	0.91	"	1.17	"	1.88	"	0.75	"	
II	0.30	"	0.13	"	....	....	0.80	"	0.71	"	0.13	"	
III	0.78	W'd	0.95	W'd	0.61	W'd	0.87	W'd	0.97	W'd	0.68	W'd	
IV	1.35	"	1.57	"	0.68	"	1.56	"	1.89	"	0.59	"	
V	1.50	"	1.77	"	0.83	"	1.89	"	2.19	"	0.57	"	
VI	1.32	"	1.62	"	0.73	"	1.56	"	1.73	"	0.50	"	
VII	1.03	"	1.19	"	0.68	"	0.62	"	0.81	"	0.69	"	
VIII	0.06	E'd	0.11	E'd	....	....	0.96	E'd	0.78	E'd	....	E'd	
IX	0.76	"	0.75	"	....	....	1.62	"	1.62	"	0.67	"	
X	1.78	"	1.55	"	0.40	"	1.92	"	1.76	"	0.84	"	
XI	2.05	"	1.93	"	1.31	"	2.15	"	2.31	"	0.97	"	

LUNAR HOUR.	STATION BETWEEN EAST AND WEST BANKS. June 24–25th, 1859.						STATION IN NARROWS. July 31 and August 1, 1858.						
	Velocity at Surface.	Dir.	Velocity at 11 Feet.	Dir.	Velocity at 31 Feet.	Dir.	Velocity at Surface.	Dir.	Velocity at 31 Feet.	Dir.	Velocity at 92 Feet.	Dir.	
0	1.08	S'd	1.07	S'd	0.02	N'd	1.56	S'd	1.45	S'd	0.20	N'd	
I	1.49	"	1.17	"	0.07	S'd	1.48	"	1.76	"	0.22	"	
II	1.76	"	1.09	"	0.25	N'd	1.51	"	1.24	"	0.55	"	
III	1.43	"	0.86	"	0.38	"	1.02	"	0.45	"	0.09	"	
IV	0.91	"	0.50	"	0.32	"	0.15	N'd	0.42	N'd	0.98	S'd	
V	0.40	N'd	0.01	N'd	0.20	"	0.52	"	0.55	"	0.85	"	
VI	0.16	"	0.64	"	0.49 (?)	"	0.86	"	0.73	"	1.48	"	
VII	0.73	"	0.91	"	0.44	"	1.03	"	1.08	"	1.93	"	
VIII	0.71	"	0.64 (?)	"	0.06	"	0.57	"	0.93	"	1.58	"	
IX	0.50	S'd	0.61	S'd	0.05	"	0.20	S'd	0.30	S'd	0.42	"	
X	0.51	"	0.40 (?)	"	0.08	"	0.81	"	0.70	"	0.19	"	
XI	0.88	"	0.89 (?)	"	0.01	N'd	1.23	"	1.23	"	0.06	"	

ED. H. FOOTE, *Computer.*

Table No. 12—Continued.

STATION OFF ROBBINS' REEF, July 7-8, 1859. — STATION BETWEEN GOVERNOR'S AND BEDLOE'S ISLANDS, Sept. 1-2, 1858.

LUNAR HOURS.	Velocity at Surface.	Dir.	Velocity at 23 feet.	Dir.	Velocity at 39 feet.	Dir.	Velocity at Surface.	Dir.	Velocity at 12 feet.	Dir.	Velocity at 34 feet.	Dir.
0	0.67	S'd.	0.97	S'd.	0.31	S'd.	1.45	S'd.	1.09	S'd.	0.31	S'd.
I	1.24	"	1.43	"	0.40	"	1.45	"	1.64	"	0.51	"
II	1.26	"	1.52	"	0.41	"	1.45	"	1.45	"	0.53	"
III	0.86	"	1.10	"	0.29	"	1.26	"	1.01	"	0.53	"
IV	0.55	"	0.55	"	0.68	"	0.91	"	0.48	"	1.66	N'd.
V	0.40	"	0.32	"	0.70	N'd.	0.38 (?)	N'd.	0.09 (?)	N'd.	1.09 (?)	"
VI	0.47	N'd.	0.41 (?)	N'd.	1.34	"	0.31 (?)	"	0.63 (?)	"	1.35 (?)	"
VII	0.06	"	0.69	"	1.12	"	0.63	"	0.84	"	1.41	"
VIII	0.25	"	1.00	"	1.05	"	0.48	"	0.81	"	1.35	"
IX	0.32	S'd.	0.71	"	0.75	"	0.12	S'd.	0.35	S'd.	1.48 (?)	S'd.
X	0.01	"	0.38	S'd.	0.15	"	0.41	"	0.53	"	0.22 (?)	"
XI	0.24	"	0.27	"	0.12	"	0.89	"	1.24	"	0.39	"

STATION OFF CASTLE GARDEN, June 22-23, 1859. — STATION OFF 41ST STREET, HUDSON RIVER, Sept. 4-5, 1858.

LUNAR HOURS.	Velocity at Surface.	Dir.	Velocity at 23 feet.	Dir.	Velocity at 39 feet.	Dir.	Velocity at Surface.	Dir.	Velocity at 12 feet.	Dir.	Velocity at 34 feet.	Dir.
0	1.20	S'd.	0.81	S'd.	0.43	S'd.	0.75	S'd.	0.71	S'd.	0.40	S'd.
I	1.73	"	1.25	"	0.69	"	1.62	"	1.00	"	0.98	"
II	1.75	"	1.32	"	0.15	"	2.15	"	2.18	"	1.44	"
III	1.69	"	1.63	"	0.22	"	1.96	"	2.04	"	0.65	N'd.
IV	1.44	"	1.09	"	0.43	"	1.43	"	1.30	"	0.05	"
V	0.98	"	0.37	"	0.41	"	0.58	"	0.39	"	0.28	"
VI	0.62	"	0.45	"	0.47	N'd.	0.60	"	0.74	"	0.86	"
VII	0.20	"	1.17	N'd.	0.55	"	0.04	N'd.	0.71	N'd.		N'd.
VIII	0.11	"	1.42	"	0.90	"	1.12	"	1.52	"	1.19	"
IX	0.17	"	1.16	"	0.65	"	1.10	"	1.46	"	1.02	"
X	0.44	"	0.37	"	0.30	"	0.89	"	1.06	"	0.65	"
XI	1.20	"	0.72	S'd.	0.19	S'd.	0.22	"	0.22	"	0.01	"

ED. H. FOOTE, *Computer.*

Table No. 13.

SPECIFIC GRAVITIES OF WATER IN THE HUDSON RIVER AT AND BELOW THE SURFACE.

Sept., 1871.　　　　REDUCED TO TEMPERATURE OF 60° FAHR.

Distance from Sandy Hook.	STATION.	END OF FLOOD CURRENT.			END OF EBB CURRENT.		
		Surface.	Below.		Surface.	Below.	
		Sp. Grav.	Depth.	Sp. Grav.	Sp. Grav.	Depth.	Sp. Grav.
Naut. miles.			*Feet.*			*Feet.*	
17½	Off 20th-street,.........	1.0198	57	1.0206	(1872) 1.0141	53	1.0181
34½	" Dobb's Ferry,......	1.0024	30	1.0114	1.0013	30	1.0022
38½	" Tarrytown, ...	1.0021	30	1.0089	1.0016	30	1.0076
43½	" Teller's Point,.....	1.0011	30	1.0087	1.0013	30	1.0087
49½	" Verplanck's Point,.	1.0012	30	1.0034	1.0014	30	1.0014
53½	" Iona Island,........	1.0017(?)	30	1.0037	1.0012	30	1.0012
56½	" Denning's Landing,	1.0016	..	1.0028	1.0012	..	1.0021
61	" Cold Spring,........	1.0015	30	1.0026	1.0010	..	....
65	" New-Windsor,.....	....	..	....	1.0006	..	....
70½	" Carthage,..........	1.0003	48	1.0016	1.0006	48	1.0012
75	" Barnegat, ...	1.0006	60	1.0006	1.0006	60	1.0006
79½	" Poughkeepsie,.....	1.0007	48	1.0007	1.0006	48	1.0005

H. L. MARINDIN, *Computer.*

Table No. 14.

CURRENTS OF EAST RIVER AT WALL STREET.

GROUPED ACCORDING TO LUNAR HOURS.

Not corrected for tide.

Lunar Hours.	Eastern Station.	Middle Station.	Western Station.	REMARKS.
	Naut. Miles.	*Naut. Miles.*	*Naut. Miles.*	
0..........	—1.07	—3.40	—3.60	Distances of Stations, from Har-
I..............	—0.38	—3 20	—3.50	beck's Wharf :
II.............	+0.36	—2.20	—2.75	
III.............	+0.50	+0.10	—0.30	Eastern Station, 350 feet.
IV..............	+1.15	+1 25	+0.80	Middle " 842 "
V...............	+1.70	+1.95	+1.50	Western " 1,320 "
VI..............	+2 10	+2.22	+1.30	Gig " 1,700 "
VII.............	+1.70	+2.40	+2.00	
VIII.	+1.50	+2.05	+1.20	To Pier No. 16, New-York, 2,000 feet.
IX..............	+0.80	+0.65	+0.15	
X..............	—1.00	—2.60	—2.60 (?)	
XI..............	—1.46	—3.20	—3.10	

Velocity, 60 feet from Pier 16, at iv. *h.* xxx. *m.* = 0.30 Nautical miles.
" at Gig station, at 0 *h.* = 3.00 " "
" 40 feet from Pier 16, at 1 *h.* = 1.45 " "
" 60 " " " 16, at 1 *h.* = 1.90 " "

H. L. MARINDIN, *Computer.*

Table No. 15.

VOLUMES PASSING THROUGH EAST RIVER AT WALL STREET SECTION.

	Distance from Harbeck's Wharf.	Mean Depth.	Area of Section.	Velocity of Stream.	Direction		Volume.	
					h.	m.		
	Feet.	*Feet.*	*Sq. feet.*	*Ft. per hour.*			*Cubic feet.*	
Flood—Easterly drift.	0 to 400	43.6	17,440	4,260	7	15	538,600,000	
	4 to 800	41.9	17,960	8,520	7	15	1,109,400,000	
	8 to 1,200	48.3	19,320	9,129	7	..	1,234,600,000	
	12 to 1,600	51.7	20,680	7,912	6	45	1,104,500,000	
	16 to 2,000	40.4	16,160	3,652	6	..	354,000,000	
		45.8	91,560	6,693	6	51	Sum of above,	= 4,341,100,000
Ebb—Westerly drift.	0 to 400	41.6	16,640	1,826	5	..	151,900,000	
	4 to 800	42.5	17,000	7,304	6	..	745,000,000	
	8 to 1,200	45.9	18,360	11,626	6	10	1,316,000,000	
	12 to 1,600	49.4	17,760	11,868	6	10	1,446,000,000	
	16 to 2,000	38.0	15,200	7,730	6	10	724,600,000	
		43.5	86,960	8,071	5	54	Sum of above,	= 4,383,500,000

Mean of Flood and Ebb,.. = 4,362,300,000

Ratios of scour, (varying with v².)
Extreme, 1 against 1.7.
Mean, 1 against 1.5.

H. MITCHELL, *Computer.*

Table No. 16.

MEAN LOW WATER SECTIONS (221 ON STAFF AT GOVERNOR'S ISLAND.)

NORTH RIVER AT FORTY-SECOND STREET, GAS HOUSE PIER END.

Distances in feet from 42d Street Wharf.	Depth at Mean Low Water.	REMARKS.
0	18.5	Bowditch Gig, 95 feet from
100	20.0	42d Street Wharf.
200	22.0	
300	24.0	
400	29.7	
500	32.5	
600	31.7	
700	35.5	
800	36.2	Schooner Bowditch, 800 feet
900	36.0	from 42d Street Wharf.
1,000	35.5	
1,100	35.5	
1,200	35.5	
1,300	35.7	
1,400	35.7	
1,500	35.7	
1,600	36.0	
1,700	36.2	
1,800	36.2	
1,900	37.5	
2,000	37.7	
2,100	38.0	
2,200	39.0	Steamer Arago, 2,200 feet
2,300	41.0	from 42d Street Wharf.
2,400	44.0	
2,500	45.2	
2,600	45.7	
2,700	46.5	
2,800	47.2	
2,900	47.5	
3,000	47.2	
3,100	46.0	
3,200	44.5	
3,300	38.0	
3,400	32.0	
3,500	26.5	
3,600	24.0	
3,700	20.0	Schooner Hassler, 3,700 feet
3,800	14.0	from 42d Street Wharf.
3,900	10.0	Hassler's Gig, 3,900 feet
4,000	5.7	from 42d Street Wharf.
4,100	4.0	
4,200	2.0	
4,300	1.2	
4,400	0.5	
4,500	0.0	End of line at Jersey Shore.
Mean.	30.34	

EAST RIVER AT WALL STREET, END OF HARBECK'S WHARF, BROOKLYN.

Distances in feet from Harbeck's Wharf.	Depth at Mean Low Water.	REMARKS.
0	22.0	Harbeck's Wharf.
100	47.2	
200	45.5	
300	42.7	Schooner Hassler, 350 feet
400	40.5	from Harbeck's Wharf.
500	40.0	
600	41.0	
700	42.3	
800	43.0	Steamer Arago, 842 feet
900	44.4	from Harbeck's Wharf.
1,000	43.5	
1,100	45.3	
1,200	48.0	
1,300	48.6	Bowditch's Gig, 1,320 feet
1,400	48.0	from Harbeck's Wharf.
1,500	48.4	
1,600	47.5	
1,700	42.5	Gig Station, 1,700 feet from
1,800	37.0	Harbeck's Wharf.
1,900	30.9	
2,000	25.4	End of Pier 16, New-York.
Mean.	41.6	

Mean Rise, 4.3.

H. L. MARINDIN,
Computer.

Table No. 17.

CURRENTS OF HUDSON RIVER, OFF 42D STREET,

SEPTEMBER 13TH AND 14TH, 1872.

Civil Time.	Velocity at Eastern Station.	Velocity at Middle Station.	Velocity at Western Station.	Civil Time.	Velocity at Eastern Station.	Velocity at Middle Station.	Velocity at Western Station.
Sept. 13							
h. m.				h. m.			
13 30	−0.25		+0.15	11 30	−2.60	−2.60	−1.45
14 00			−0.55	12 00	−2.65	−2.65	−1.25
14 30	+0.15	+0.10	−0.75	12 30	−2.57	−2.57	−1.05
15 00	−0.45	+0.62	+0.95	13 00	−2.30	−2.30	−0.85
15 30	+0.80	+1.00	+1.10	13 30	−2.00	−2.00	−0.57
16 00	+1.32	+1.60	+1.25	14 00	−1.52	−1.52	−0.36
16 30	+1.60	+1.90	+1.17	14 30	−1.00	−1.00	−0.20
17 00	+1.65	+2.00	+1.10	15 00	−0.35	−0.35	+0.20
17 30	+1.50	+1.92	+1.05	15 30	+0.30	+0.30	+0.55
18 00	+1.32	+1.80	+1.05				
18 30	+1.05	+1.65	+0.95				
19 00	+0.70	+1.40	+0.52				
19 30	+0.05	+0.92	+0.20				
20 00	−0.40	+0.45	−0.15				
20 30	−0.75	−0.25	−0.62				
21 00	−1.05	−1.05	−0.90				
21 30	−1.65	−1.65	−1.25				
22 00	−2.00	−2.00	−1.45				
22 30	−2.35	−2.35	−1.50				
23 00	−2.65	−2.65	−1.42				
23 30	−2.57	−2.90	−1.35				
0 00	−2.40	−2.85	−1.37				
0 30	−2.30	−2.47	−1.25				
1 00	−2.25	−2.25	−1.10				
1 30	−2.00	−2.00	−0.67				
2 00	−1.65	−1.65	−0.45				
2 30	−1.30	−1.30	−0.30				
3 00	−0.80	−0.80	−0.13				
3 30	−0.47	−0.47	+0.02				
4 00	−0.20	−0.20	+0.17				
4 30	+0.15	+0.15	+0.42				
5 00	+0.37	+0.37	+0.70				
5 30	+0.47	+0.60	+1.00				
6 00	+0.50	+0.90	+1.00				
6 30	+0.47	+1.05	+0.92				
7 00	+0.25	+0.90	+0.77				
7 30	0.00	+0.65	+0.48				
8 00	−0.15	+0.40	+0.15				
8 30	−0.30	−0.10	−0.17				
9 00	−0.75	−0.75	−0.55				
9 30	−1.20	−1.20	−1.00				
10 00	−1.65	−1.65	−1.25				
10 30	−2.00	−2.00	−1.45				
11 00	−2.42	−2.42	−1.52				

REMARKS.—Sketch D. illustrates these tables. Distances of Stations from Gas House Wharf

Gig Station,	....	95 feet
Eastern Station,	... .	800 "
Middle "	....	2,200 "
Western "	....	3,700 "
Gig "	....	3,900 "

GROUPED ACCORDING TO LUNAR HOURS.

Lunar Hours.	Velocity at Eastern Station.	Velocity at Middle Station.	Velocity at Western Station.
0.....	−1.57	−1.39	−1.10
I.....	−2.32	−2.15	−1.47
II.....	−2.63	−2.72	−1.35
III.....	−2.35	−2.46	−1.12
IV.....	−1.82	−1.83	−0.40
V.....	−0.93	−0.83	−0.01
VI.....	−0.09	+0.14	+0.35
VII.....	+0.74	+0.89	+0.85
VIII.....	+1.05	+1.24	+1.05
IX.....	+0.85	+1.35	+1.00
X.....	+0.22	+0.98	+0.36
XI.....	−0.50	−0.04	−0.40

REMARKS.—Velocities at Gig Station, 95 feet from Wharf, at—

VIII h.	+	0.55.
I h.	−	1.25.
II h.	−	1.10.

Gig Station, 3,900 feet, at—

VIII h.	+	0.67.
IX h.	+	0.50.
II h.	−	0.70.

H. L. MARINDIN, *Computer.*